PEOPLE. *UGH.*

Humorous and insightful
stories for those who are
easily annoyed by others

MJ WILSON

CONTENTS

5 INTRODUCTION

6 BECAUSE I SAID SO,
   THAT'S WHY

13 DO YOU SEE WHAT I
    SEE?

27 I SWEAR, IF YOU ASK ME
    THAT ONE MORE TIME …

39 NO … SERIOUSLY. GO
    AWAY. *PLEASE.*

46 ABOUT THE AUTHOR

*The difference between a smart man
and a dumb man?*

*One believes that he is while the other
believes he is not.*

INTRODUCTION

PEOPLE. *UGH.* contains four short stories from my book *Beef Stew for the Mind.*

I put this collection together for those of you who are tired of nosy, loud, talkative, irreverent, rude, judgmental, condescending, pretentious, arrogant, mean, clueless, wasteful, holier-than-thou, ignorant, disruptive and generally annoying people.

It is my hope that you find a little humor and insight in these stories, as well as some relief in knowing that you are not alone.

Others feel your pain, too.

-MJ Wilson

Because I Said So, *That's* Why

You can't control the speed of the rollercoaster, or the height of the hill, but you <u>can</u> decide if you choose to ride

---

Whether you're 28 or 88, once you're an adult, you're an adult. You don't have to wait until you reach a certain age or obtain a certain status to begin to say no to things you just don't want to do or be a part of. A simple "No" will do, and if anyone asks why, just say, "Because I said so, that's why."

The following is a list of several things that I absolve you from being a part of, anytime, anyplace, should you prefer to.

And please notice I said, "should you prefer to." If you desire to be a part of any of the following, that's certainly up to you.

1. **Any management position**
   (Definition of a manager: person who has to deal with everyone's sh*t, yet doesn't get paid nearly enough for doing so.)

2. **New clothing styles**
   (Live long enough and it all comes back around anyway … trust me.)

3. **Any non-mandatory event scheduled to take place before 10 a.m.**
   (What could possibly be so important so early that couldn't happen after a nice lunch?)

4. **Any outing that involves bug spray**
   (If you have to spray something *on* to keep something off …)

5. **Theme Parks**
   (What's wrong with a regular park? Why do you need a theme? Go for a walk instead. It's cheaper and better for your heart.)

6. **Any sporting event you don't give a damn about**
   (Who cares if the whole town shuts down when the local team plays? Unless that team is paying your rent, you don't have to go!)

7. **Office Parties / Christmas Parties**
   (Insert yawn here.)

8. Birthday Parties
(Yes, the individual *does* matter, but your attendance won't if you just send cash ☺)

9. Local festivals that charge more money for parking than entering
(However, you may want to sneak your kid in long enough to bring back some funnel cakes! *Yuuuuummmmmy!*)

10. Any movie with the number 2 in its title
(You and I both know they're never as good as the first. Just rent or buy it later and spare yourself the $15 for a *small* cola.)

11. Any diet that doesn't allow coffee or chocolate
(WTH?)

12. **Dinner dates with other couples**
    (Do I have to explain this one?)

13. **Expensive church services**
    (If they got a cover charge – aka "love offering" – when you enter and three more offerings before you leave ...)

14. **Reunions**
    (Thanks to Facebook, you already know who's divorced, how fat they are, and their favorite TV show.)

15. **Weddings**
    (Especially if there's A LOT of singing during the ceremony and no open bar at the reception!)

16. **Major family vacations**
    (If your family vacation requires an agenda, meeting times and a budget, it's not a vacation –

it's a second job. Stay home and play ball with the kids in the backyard instead. Not only is it cheaper, but it's also an ancient ritual called "being a family.")

17. **Conferences for your job**
(Unless they're two or more hours away and in a really cool city, they're just an extended version of your already annoying job.)

18. **Baby Showers**
(See "Birthday Parties" listed previously)

19. **Sleeping accommodations**
(Don't believe the hype – a "pull-out couch" is *NOT* a bed!)

20. **"Chipping in" at the office for a stupid gift**
(Stop throwing your money away on people you wouldn't even go bowling with.)

So there you have it – 20 things you can now say NO to and use what would've been a huge waste of your time in a much more productive way ... like sleeping!

Enjoy your new freedom.

-MJ Wilson

Do You See What I See?

Stupidity is like an object in motion: It will stay in motion with the same speed and in the same direction unless acted upon by an external force

---

Take a quick scroll through your favorite social media site or local community chat room/forum and you'll likely turn up one or more of these problems listed below:

#1 AND WE WONDER WHY THE SCHOOL LEVY NEVER PASSES – My husband and I recently moved here and enrolled our kids in the local school system. Apparently, some moron approved by the board decided to draw up the plans for the new student drop-off zone at our school. This "expert" has us (the parents) in our cars competing with the morning school buses and their drivers for the best place to allow our kids/students to enter the building. It's an accident just waiting to happen (my son was almost hit twice already) and it's extremely difficult to leave once you've dropped your child off due to the traffic jam it causes.

Educated people everywhere and they chose this guy and this design to improve our school?

-Brooke / Arkansas

#2 DUMB IDEA + DUMB DECISION = DUMB RESULTS – It's one of our community's busiest intersections. Let's put a gas station and/or pharmacy on *each* of the four corners. Then, in less than a year, they can all slowly go out of business while competing with one another. Soon after we'll have four unsightly buildings with boards over the windows, dilapidated advertisements and weeds growing all around to add to the "beauty" of our already struggling community.

Oh wait … we did that already … on the next street over.

-Shelby / Kentucky

#3 THE (RICH SCHOOL) MONEY PIT –

How about the school district I live in … incredible football fields and sports facilities, a $400 student-athlete annual participation fee, and coaching salaries that dwarf nearby school districts. Yet we're constantly bombarded with school levies, the threat of classes being cut (art, gym, music and band), and we can't get air-conditioning in two of our older elementary schools. Our classrooms are over-crowded, or faculty is under-staffed, and our teachers don't even get a planning period during their workday. To make matters worse, with all that money from the participation fees, somehow we still end up with high-school students "volunteering" as referees to officiate elementary games, and our team "uniforms" (a cheap t-shirt with a number and your child's last name on the back) still costs an *additional* $20!

But don't get me wrong ... I'm sure "Education comes FIRST" in our district. I mean, why else would our superintendent get ANOTHER raise???

-Vince / Florida

#4 BASS ACKWARDS BUSINESS – Whatever you do, do NOT let any prominent businesses come into your small town and build a few restaurants or local tourist attractions (especially if you have a town near the water or full of history like ours). No ... that would make too much sense. Don't use your brain or anything.

Instead, do what our town did: Take your busiest or most historical street, tear down all major landmarks and cultural icons, and install used-car lots and storage buildings in their place. This way, two local business owners profit a little while the rest of the town suffers greatly.

Absolutely ridiculous.

Our leadership doesn't seem to get it. Remaining a small town doesn't mean remaining a "stuck" town. Despite popular belief, we *can* grow without losing our charm. Don't believe me? Check out Port Townsend, Washington.

-Valerie / Oregon

#5 THE (UNGODLY) GODLY – I've been attending the same church now for the last seven years. One thing I've noticed that increasingly disturbs me is how we *continue* to ask for money for our Building Fund (despite never needing it) and our Community Fund (despite never using it).

Our Building Fund is supposedly in place so we can increase the size of our church (to accommodate its growth when necessary) and the Community Fund is supposedly for community emergencies and/or benefits (relief for local victims of natural disasters, food for the needy, or to help the community in a positive way). Yet for as long as I've been here, we've spent thousands of dollars increasing the *size* of our church – bigger sanctuary, new gymnasium, more seating – despite its lack of growth (we have fewer attendees now than when I started) and we're remodeling our pastor's office ... *again!* (This time we're adding on a private kitchen ... apparently the break room just down the hall from his office is too far to walk.)

Worse, we still have never done *anything* for the local community! I mean *nothing*! No free oil changes for single moms, no free legal advice for those going through divorce, no lawn service for the elderly, no donations to the local parks and playgrounds, no food pantry, no homeless shelter … *Nothing.*

If you ask me, the question shouldn't be, "What would Jesus do?" The real question is, *"What would Jesus do about what we are not doing?"*

-Carlos / Nevada

#6 … AND THE FORTY THIEVES – In my city, local police and firefighters are driving police cars and fire trucks that lack modern equipment. These brave men and women risk their lives – burglaries, gang fights, burning buildings – with technology that's outdated or in disrepair. Each year they beg for donations to improve their safety and ours. Yet at the same time, our local and state governments continue to spend thousands and thousands of dollars (taxpayers' dollars I might add) on anything from new leather-bound chairs and oak desks for their offices to limousine services and tickets to the local symphony. (Did I mention this was from taxpayers' money and NOT from their own income?)

Ironically, several of these politicians promised lower crime and increased public safety while running for office. Unfortunately, the only thing that's gotten lower is the amount of money these jerks have to spend out of their own pockets.

-Antonio / California

IN ~~EINSTEIN'S~~ MY OWN WORDS – Regardless of *how* these problems are brought to our attention – sarcastic complaints, social whining or legitimate concern – it doesn't dismiss the fact that these problems are ... well ... *still problems.*

They *do* exist in several of our communities.

They *are* affecting us in a negative way.

And they *can* be reviewed, questioned and or even investigated.

Keeping this in mind, I'd like you to go back and reread each problem I listed previously. (Yes, all six of them.) And when you do, forget about *how* they're told to you and think about *what* they're telling you.

Do they sound familiar? Are any of them happening in your church? Your school district? Your community?

Do you even know?

I don't say that to be rude or condescending. *I'm serious.* Do you even know what's going on in the world around you? Are you aware of what's (possibly) happening right under your nose on a daily basis that's affecting you in a negative way?

I realize most of us have so much going on at any given moment that the last thing we feel like making time for is attending our local school-board meeting, voting in the next town-hall election, or doing a little research to find out where our donations are going.

But maybe we should.

Or if nothing else, the least we could do is start looking around and asking questions. This process doesn't have to be difficult or intense, it just needs to be started.

Let's start questioning our current methods. Let's take a serious look at their validity. And let's investigate who, what, when, where, how and why.

Your city:
- Does it really take a *zillion* orange barrels and two years of road construction to fix a two-mile stretch of road? Seriously? Could there be something else going on here you don't know about?

Your county:
- Am I wrong or isn't the guy running for treasurer in your county the same guy who was caught embezzling thousands of dollars from his previous place of employment? And this doesn't seem a little strange to you?

Your church:
- Do you really need to remodel your offices every 3-5 years? Does the carpet in the sanctuary really need replaced ... again? Isn't there a low-income housing community just a few miles

away or a local family or two who could desperately use your help – financially or otherwise?

Your local school district:

- Your superintendent got another raise because why??? And who's planning the school budget so poorly that every five years you have to pass *another* levy? Are levies really the *only* way to raise money for schools? Where's all the money from the sports programs going?

Your community:

- Why did they cut down all the trees along the main road? Were they in the way or something? And did your town really need another used car lot or over-sized parking lot put in? Why not a new park, library or public media center? Who made these decisions and why?

Your world:

- You tell me ... What's a good question to ask???

Now before you send me an email explaining why your church or school or other "thing" needs whatever I've questioned above, I want you to realize, I did NOT say that these places or organizations *don't* need these things, I *asked* if they do. I honestly don't know what's relevant to your respective area and what's not – that's why I asked. And that's all I'm hoping you'll begin to do – start asking.

Maybe your church *does* need new carpet. Maybe your town *does* need another gas station – I honestly have no idea. Only you can answer those questions and I hope you'll do whatever it takes to do so.

Remember, it only takes one to get the ball rolling.

Don't be afraid to investigate. Don't be afraid to ask questions.

Or as I started to write at the beginning of my response and will do so now: In the words of Albert Einstein, "The important thing is to not stop questioning."

Pretty simple advice, I know. But it was given to us by a man who became a genius, not because he had all the answers, but because he never stopped looking for them. *And neither should you.*

Keep investigating.

Keep asking questions.

And yes, keep looking.

-MJ Wilson

I Swear, If You Ask Me That One More Time ...

Those who can, do. Those who can't, annoy those who can

Okay, before you jump into this story, you have to know the background that comes with it. So check this out ...

I sent this story off to Fred (my editor), so he could proofread it. Normally, I get these stories back with a ton of red marks for using improper grammar, etc., but nothing major. However, this time his feedback was *quite* different. Different enough that I thought it was worth sharing.

This is literally, word-for-word, what he sent back to me:

Wilson – What does this section serve as? I know it shows how rude people can be to ask these questions (and points out other faults they have) ... but some of the responses are pretty mean-spirited. Now don't get me wrong: I enjoy the sass throughout this. And I do see the value in the comic relief this section provides. But most of your vignettes provide life lessons – points for readers to ponder.

Do these responses fit with the theme of your book?

(Just wanted you to ruminate on the purpose here.)

After I read Fred's comments, I'd like to say that I took his advice and corrected everything accordingly. But truth be told, the first thing I did was look up the word "ruminate" to see what it means! (Hey, I may have a master's degree, but it's not like I say "ruminate" on a daily basis, here!) After doing so (and laughing at myself in the process), I found that it means, *"to reflect deeply on a subject."*

Okay, so Fred wants me to "reflect deeply" on this story and perhaps think twice about adding it to the Beef Stew stories, right? (Or at a minimum, at least know why I'm adding it.) And after much thought (or ruminating!) I decided the purpose of this story is to show you, the reader, that you are not alone when it comes to being asked annoying questions. We all get them and we all wanna punch the people who ask them right in the throat, right? (Okay, maybe not literally, but you can't tell me you haven't thought about it at least once!)

So here's your comic relief. A survey of nine of the most annoying questions we all hear, along with the brilliant and sometimes sarcastic answers suggested by a few of my friends from across the country.

Feel free to "ruminate" over these the next time *you* wanna punch someone right in the throat! And although they're not to be taken too seriously, always remember: There's typically a little bit of truth in even the simplest joke. So pay attention!

P.S. #7 and #9 are *my* favorites! I about choked on my food when I read them.

Annoying Question #1
HOW MUCH MONEY DO YOU MAKE?

Answer: *Apparently not enough or I wouldn't still be hanging out with you.* Listen honey, it's none of your business how much money I make. Besides, why do you want to know? What are you possibly going to do with this information? Help me invest? Perhaps donate to my child's college fund? *Yeah* *right.* You and I both know the only reason you wanna know how much money I make is so you'll know how much you wanna borrow from me!

I'm sorry I worked so hard for my financial status. Had I known sitting on my ass and doing nothing while waiting for "Mr. Right" to show up was a career choice, perhaps we'd both be on the same busted-up playing field right now.

-Michelle / Washington, D.C.

Annoying Question #2
YOU MEAN YOU'RE *STILL* NOT MARRIED YET?

Answer: You mean you're still not divorced yet? Listen, just because you're in a miserable marriage and don't have the guts to get out, it doesn't mean I need to rush into a marriage so you can feel better about yours. I'm in no hurry to "settle down" like you. Believe me. *I'm single, not desperate.*

-Tyler / Omaha, NE

Annoying Question #3
SHOULDN'T YOU BE DONE WITH YOUR DEGREE BY NOW?

Answer: HELLO! IT'S A FOUR-YEAR PROGRAM! And that's only if I go full-time – which I'm not, because I can't! I'm barely into year number three! YOU try working 40 hours a week, managing two kids AND going back to school. *It ain't easy.*

And don't be hatin' on me either! Just because you dropped out and never went back doesn't mean I can't go back or won't finish! I WILL finish and I WILL graduate. I don't care if it takes me 10 years! Just remember, we aren't getting any younger. And at our age, I think it's pretty obvious the only one falling behind in this scenario is YOU.

-Shannon / Des Moines, IA

Annoying Question #4
DIDN'T YOU ALREADY TRY THIS DIET ONCE BEFORE?

Answer: And? Is there something wrong with trying it again? Maybe I feel more confident this time. Maybe I feel better about the plan. Maybe I failed the first time and wanna try again. At least I'm trying, which is better than doing *nothing* about my weight, or my looks, or my career … *like you.*

-Tonya / Dover, DE

Annoying Question #5
WHEN ARE YOU TWO GONNA HAVE SOME BABIES? DON'T YOU WANT CHILDREN?

Answer: We will have babies WHEN we want babies, IF we want babies! And we're certainly not having them for you! Just because you had all four of your children by the time you were 26 doesn't mean we're falling behind. We want to live as a couple FIRST and as parents second. We may wait until we're both over 30. Maybe 35. Maybe not at all. But believe me, if and when we do have babies, trust me, you'll be the first one … no scratch that … we'll probably *never* tell you. Seriously.

-Mitchell & Nicole / Minneapolis, MN

Annoying Question #6
WHY ARE YOU STILL SMOKING? DON'T YOU KNOW IT'S BAD FOR YOU?

Answer: Gee … let me think for a minute … Wow. *No. I did not know smoking was bad for me. I had no idea.* All this time wasted. If I had only known, perhaps I could've easily overcome my ADDICTION TO NICOTINE and the feeling of "escape" that my cigarette gives me when people like YOU come around, asking me stupid, annoying questions!

Of course I know it's bad for me.

But rather than remind me CONSTANTLY, why don't you try to understand why I do it? Has it ever occurred to you that maybe I actually DO wanna quit, and have a plan to do so in my own time? It's a lot harder than you think.

If you're truly concerned, why don't you try helping me find a solution to this problem instead of simply telling me the result if I don't?

-Levi / Memphis, TN

Annoying Question #7
YOU LOOK TIRED. ARE YOU OKAY?

Answer: Oh yeah … I'm good. I was just up all night with your mom.

-Miguel / Albuquerque, NM

Annoying Question #8
ARE YOU *STILL* WORKING THAT BUSINESS OF YOURS? WEREN'T YOU SUPPOSED TO BE RICH BY NOW?

Answer: Are you *STILL* working 40 hours a week at a job you hate? At least I'm doing something about my financial state instead of making fun of others'. You're so busy comparing where I am to where you are … Why don't you compare where I'm headed to where you'll be?

Oh wait … I'm sorry. I forgot. That might require admitting one of us is following his dream while the other is just dreaming.

-Scott / Seattle, WA

Annoying Question #9
DO YOU HAVE ANY CASH I CAN BORROW? I'M BROKE UNTIL NEXT WEEK.

Answer: Oh my gosh! YOU? BROKE??? NO WAAAAY! I just can't believe it! Seems like just the other day you were … No, wait … you're right. You ARE broke. Broke-minded, broke lifestyle, broke friendships.

Let me ask you, when are you *not* broke? You know damn well you and I make the same amount of money. We were hired on the same day and work at the same call center. The only difference between you and me is you blow your money trying to keep up an image you can't afford (Miss "Fake it 'til you make it") while I save my money trying to live within my means.

Stop buying new shoes every week. Stop buying a new cell phone every six months. And stop blaming the Devil every time your electric gets cut off. Last time I checked it was your jobless, classless, live-in boyfriend who was taking all your money, *not Satan*.

-Kelsey / Denver, CO

No ... Seriously. Go Away. *Please.*

Stop listening to what they're telling you and start looking at what they're actually giving you

Have you seen the sign that some neighborhoods are now posting? The one that says, "*NO SOLICITING – We are too broke to buy anything – We know who we are voting for – and we have found Jesus – Seriously, unless you're selling Thin Mint cookies, Please GO AWAY!!!*"

As funny as this may sound (I got a good laugh out of it the first time I read it, too), it has a lot of truth to it.

The majority of my neighbors and I are well over 50 years of age. We have kids *and* grandkids, which means we're always attending birthday parties, donating to the kids' soccer teams, helping with rent or covering somebody's school loan. We have money, yes. But we have family and they have needs, and bills, and "life."

We have our educations and political sense, and have had them for quite some time. We know how to vote, when to vote and who we want to vote for. And despite your judgments, we consider ourselves to be good people, if not Godly people.

We've seen and heard just about everything. And after 50+ years on this planet, one thing we typically don't see is the action to back up the statement. So rather than coming to our doors, telling us what we should be doing, buying, saving or giving, how 'bout you show us instead?

For instance …

Stop telling us we need to buy your products, try your services or donate to your cause.

If you're so interested in getting our money, why not demonstrate how you spend yours?

SHOW US where you've paid the rent for someone less fortunate.

SHOW US where you've given away gas cards or free groceries to a needy family.

SHOW US where you've sponsored a local student so that he or she can afford to play sports.

Anything that would cause us to believe giving our earned income to you would be better than keeping it ourselves. You do *that*, and not only would we be more willing to give, but we might actually buy your products, too.

Stop telling us who to vote for.

If you know who we should vote for then obviously you know our property taxes are too high, the police are under-staffed, and the school levy never passes. So why not take the time you're wasting going door-to-door asking for our votes/support, and instead, use it to find a way to solve one or more of the problems I just listed above.

You do *that* and we just might vote for you or your candidate next election.

Stop telling us we need to go to your church.

Has it ever dawned on you that just because we don't go to *your* church, it doesn't mean we don't go at all?

Rather than wasting money on catchy fliers and large billboards telling us why we need to come to your house of worship, why don't you stop coming to ours, and instead, do what Jesus did (or would do) – you know ... feed the hungry (donate food to a poor family in our community), heal the sick (or at least pay someone's medical bills), offer free school supplies for low-income families, or find a young man trying to better his life through college and help him afford a tutor or financial aid. (Do I really need to tell you the problems we all face?)

Stop telling us what to do and start showing us that you are already doing it. You do *that* and not only would we come to your church, we'd volunteer to help you accomplish those tasks.

We are tired of the same old unfulfilled promises, political pageantry and religious rhetoric. But that doesn't mean we don't want to help. It just means until you show us what you're doing instead of telling us what to do, we don't believe working with you is the answer.

Trust me, we don't need a miracle ...
Just a reason to believe one could
happen.

-Richard / Detroit, MI

PEOPLE. *UGH.*

About the Author

MJ Wilson is a Self-Help
Author & Speaker

HOW IT ALL STARTED

A teacher in both public and private schools for 15 years, Wilson came to the conclusion that the biggest problem facing students wasn't academics, but rather, relationships, self-esteem and inspiration. It was at this time he decided to make the world his classroom, rather than his classroom his world. So with an outdated computer and the last penny from his savings, Wilson left his comfortable teaching career behind and set off to fulfill his dream of becoming a best-selling author and inspirational speaker.

CAREER AS AUTHOR & SPEAKER

Although first known for his book *The Best College Student Survival Guide Ever Written* (2013), and as a motivator of college students, after much success and several emotional, heart-felt speaking engagements, it was clear to him "You can't teach people if you can't reach people." And from that understanding (and passion to help others) *Beef Stew for the Mind* was born.

Now, with his career beginning to flourish, Wilson has already begun work on *Beef Stew for the Mind – Vol. 2* and hopes to make it into a continual series. He's also currently working on a children's book, has plans to write several relationship and dating guides, and will be starting his own YouTube channel soon.

PERSONAL NOTES

MJ Wilson, who holds a master's degree in education, is also a certified fitness instructor who enjoys music (especially old-school hip-hop), traveling and the occasional karaoke opportunity.

An Ohio native, he now resides in Tampa, Florida.

If you would like MJ Wilson to speak to your organization, or need more information about his books and services, please visit his website.

PEOPLE. *UGH.*

MJ-Wilson.com

Facebook.com/AuthorMJWilson

AuthorMJWilson

@AuthorMJWilson

Get the book
that started it all ...

IF CHICKEN SOUP FOR THE SOUL OPENED YOUR HEART

BEEF
STEW
FOR THE MIND

WILL OPEN YOUR EYES

MJ WILSON

Because life's too short
to be unhappy and
too long to be miserable

*Purchase at Amazon.com
or MJ-Wilson.com*

Don't just go
to college ...

GRADUATE!

Purchase at Amazon.com or MJ-Wilson.com

Made in the USA
Middletown, DE
04 November 2017